3/4

EARLY AMERICAN CULTURE

BY CATHERINE NICHOLS

Rourke
Publishing LLC
Vero Beach, Florida 32964

Developed by Nancy Hall, Inc., for Rourke Publishing.
© 2006 Nancy Hall, Inc.

Acknowledgments are listed on page 48.

www.rourkepublishing.com

Photo research by L. C. Casterline
Design by Atif Toor and Iram Khandwala

Library of Congress Cataloging-In-Publication Data

Nichols, Catherine.
  Early American culture / by Catherine Nichols.
     p. cm. -- (Discovering the arts)
  ISBN 1-59515-518-X (hardcover)
  1. Arts, American--Juvenile literature. I. Title. II. Series.
  NX503.5.N53 2006
  709'.73--dc22
                          2005010734

Title page: *The United States Capitol*, ca. 1800, by William Russell Birch.
In August 1814, the British burned the first Capitol building. Congress almost decided
to move to another city but stayed when banks provided a $500,000 loan to rebuild.

Printed in the USA
10 9 8 7 6 5 4 3 2 1

CONTENTS

A NEW WORLD

When the first Europeans came to North America to live, they didn't have much time for art. They were too busy surviving. They had land to clear and homes to build. They had to hunt animals and grow crops. They suffered through long, cold winters.

Even though they were living in a new country, the colonists still considered themselves European. The houses they built looked like the houses they had left behind. Their furniture and the clothes they wore looked similar, too. The first theaters performed mostly English plays. There were no art schools, so artists went to Europe to study painting. Slowly, this began to change as the colonists established themselves in the New World and

In colonial days, anyone who had a musket carried a powder horn to hold their gunpowder. Made out of cow or ox horns, the powder horns were often carved. This one was made about 1757. It shows New York City (at bottom), as well as the Hudson and Mohawk River valleys, Lake Champlain, and Lake Ontario.

Liberty in the Form of the Goddess of Youth: Giving Support to the Bald Eagle, 1796, by Edward Savage. In this **engraving**, the bald eagle is a symbol of the newly formed United States of America. This image was very popular in its day, and many prints were made from the engraving.

began to **prosper**. These people were proud of their toughness. This pride and newfound independence led to the American Revolution and the forming of the United States of America. Now the people were no longer colonists but Americans.

By the early 1800s, the country had doubled its size. America had its own federal style of architecture. There was a **distinct** American literature that included novels, nonfiction, poetry, and plays. The Library of Congress was established in Washington, D.C. There were art schools in New York and Philadelphia. And in the 1820s, America gave birth to its first **notable** artistic style, the Hudson River School. America was prospering, and so were the arts.

CHAPTER 1

COMING TO AMERICA

In 1565, Spanish settlers founded St. Augustine, Florida, the first colony in the United States. Twenty years later, the first British colonists settled on Roanoke Island in Virginia. Among the colonists were Thomas Hariot and John White. Hariot was an explorer and a scientist, and White was an artist. Their job was to record the unfamiliar people, plants, and animals they found in the New World.

Hariot and White returned to England when the colony was deserted in 1586.

Village of Secoton, 1585, by John White.
In his watercolor of a Native American village,
White included a religious ceremony (lower right).
He also showed three fields, one of newly sprouted
corn, one of young plants, and one of ripe corn.

The Arrival of the Englishmen in Virginia, 1590, engraving by Theodor de Bry.

Two years later, Hariot published *A Briefe and True Report of the New Found Land of Virginia.*

The first two Virginia colonies failed. Finally, in 1607, Captain John Smith led 104 colonists in settling Jamestown. Though many of the settlers died, more arrived in January 1609, and the colony survived.

The English explorer Henry Hudson claimed the area around the Hudson River for the Dutch in 1609. The colony was named New Netherland. The capital of New Amsterdam was founded after the Dutch purchased Manhattan Island from the Iroquois in 1624. Within 50 years, it would fall to the English and become New York.

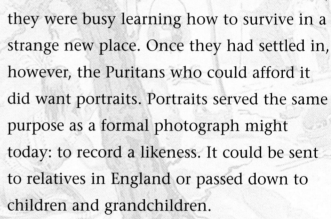

Elizabeth Clarke Freake (Mrs. John Freake) and Baby Mary, ca. 1674, by an unknown artist. The Puritans did not always dress plainly or in dark clothes. This can be seen in Mrs. Freake's jewelry and in the ribbons, lace, and embroidery on her and her child's clothes.

Farther north, the Pilgrims who sailed on the *Mayflower* in 1620 founded Plymouth Colony in Massachusetts. Ten years later, another group of Puritans settled the Massachusetts Bay Colony. Both groups were seeking a place where they could worship as they pleased.

Art held little interest for the Puritans. Like other colonists, they were busy learning how to survive in a strange new place. Once they had settled in, however, the Puritans who could afford it did want portraits. Portraits served the same purpose as a formal photograph might today: to record a likeness. It could be sent to relatives in England or passed down to children and grandchildren.

In colonial times, portrait painters were called **limners**. Most of them worked at other jobs to support themselves. Many limners had no formal training in art. Nor were there any museums filled with Old Masters they could copy. Some limners, however, may have seen reproductions (copies) of European artwork. The limners' style was two-dimensional, or flat, and their sitters often looked stiff and formal.

Wealthy Puritans did not mind showing off their **status**. They thought their success meant that God approved of them. Their good clothes were often colorful and decorated with lace and embroidery. Skillful craftsmen turned out fine furniture, decorated with carvings and inlaid wood, and **upholstered** in fine fabrics.

This cupboard was made of oak and pine in Hadley, Massachusetts, between 1710 and 1720 for Hannah Barnard, whose name appears on the upper section.

Stonecutters decorated the Puritans' gravestones with symbols of death, as well as life and rebirth. Elizabeth Raynsford died in 1688 and was buried in the King's Chapel Burying Ground, the oldest cemetery in Boston. A winged death's head, or skull, is carved on the top of her tombstone. A skull alone stood for death, which comes to all people. With wings, it stood for the soul departing from the body.

Education was important to the Puritans. In 1635, they opened the Boston Latin School, the first public school in America. The following year, Harvard College was founded. Both girls and boys could attend primary school, but only men went on to higher education.

Anne Bradstreet was educated in England. She sailed to Massachusetts with her

husband in 1630. While her husband traveled on business, Bradstreet stayed home to care for and educate their eight children. She also wrote poetry. Bradstreet meant for only her family to read her poems; however, her brother-in-law showed some of them to a

This engraving shows the Harvard College campus as it looked in 1726.

publisher in London. In 1650, her poems came out in a book called *The Tenth Muse, Lately Sprung Up in America.* In 1678, six years after Bradstreet's death, the book was published in America.

The children of early America learned to read with hornbooks. Paper was expensive and tore easily, so it had to be protected. Hornbooks were wooden paddles with a sheet of paper glued on. The paper was covered with a piece of cow's horn. The horn was thin enough to let the children see the text, yet sturdy enough to protect the paper.

America's first printing press was set up at Harvard in 1638. Stephen Daye, the press's first operator, printed *The Whole Booke of Psalmes Faithfully Translated into English Metre*, also known as the *Bay Psalm Book*, in 1640. It was the first book printed and published in the colonies.

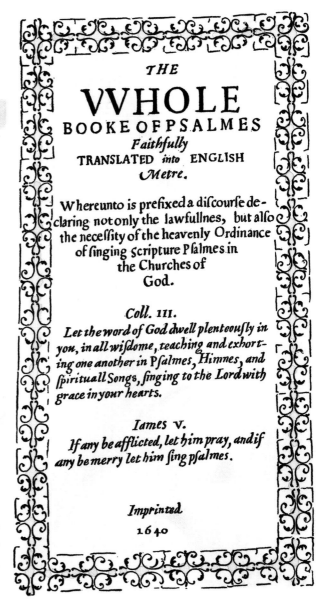

THE
VVHOLE
BOOKE OF PSALMES
Faithfully
TRANSLATED *into* ENGLISH
Metre.

Whereunto is prefixed a difcourfe declaring not only the lawfullnes, but alfo the neceffity of the heavenly Ordinance of finging fcripture Pfalmes in the Churches of God.

Coll. III.
Let the word of God dwell plenteoufly in you, in all wifdome, teaching and exhorting one another in Pfalmes, Himnes, and fpirituall Songs, finging to the Lord with grace in your hearts.

Iames V.
If any be afflicted, let him pray, and if any be merry let him fing pfalmes.

Imprinted
1640

Early colonial houses were much like the ones the colonists had left behind. In New England, "saltbox" houses were two stories high. In the back, the steep roof extended down to cover a lean-to kitchen. More well-to-do colonists often had two-story houses built with two rooms on each floor and a chimney in the center.

In Virginia, wealthy tobacco planters owned most of the land. Many of the workers were **indentured servants**, convicts, or others who agreed to work for several years in exchange for a new start in a new place. In 1619, the first Africans were brought to Virginia by force and enslaved. Here, as in New England, portraits were the only paintings in demand.

The Dock Street Theatre was built in Charleston, South Carolina, in 1736. It was the first building in

In England, houses had once been taxed on the area of ground they sat on. Since the second story didn't touch the ground, it could be larger without increasing taxes. Even though there was no such tax in the colonies, some houses, including the John Ward house, were still built this way.

America meant only for theatrical productions. Its plays were all popular English comedies and tragedies. In 1767, *The Prince of Parthia*, by Thomas Godfrey, was performed at the Southwark Theatre in Philadelphia. This was the first play written by an American to be professionally produced.

Henry Darnall III, ca. 1715, Justus Engelhardt Kühn. Note the young slave, the first African American included in a colonial painting. Though he is nicely dressed, he wears a silver collar around his neck.

The College of William and Mary was built in Williamsburg, Virginia, in 1695. The name of the architect has been lost. It is clear, however, that he based his design on buildings by the English architect Christopher Wren. He may have seen Wren's designs in pattern books imported from England. These books contained plans by famous European architects.

Bishop George Berkeley, ca. 1727, by John Smibert. Smibert came to the colonies as part of a group led by George Berkeley. They planned to set up a missionary college on the island of Bermuda, but the plans fell through.

John Smibert was the first European trained as an artist to settle in the United States. He arrived in Newport, Rhode Island, in 1729. Smibert soon moved to Boston. He couldn't earn a living by painting portraits, so he also ran a store where he sold art supplies. He formed a **partnership** with an engraver named Peter Pelham. Smibert would paint a portrait, then Pelham would produce prints of the portrait to sell in the store.

The Friends, also called Quakers, believed in peace, equality, simple living, and community. Badly treated by the Puritans, many Quakers flocked to the colonies of West Jersey and Pennsylvania. Early Quakers thought the arts were too **worldly** and did not practice them.

Benjamin West was an **exception**. The son of a Quaker innkeeper outside Philadelphia, West showed artistic talent even as a child. With no formal training, he was already working as a portrait artist by age 18. West wanted to create **history paintings** but felt he needed to study the **Old Masters**. In 1760, at the age of 22, West left for Italy. Three years later, he settled in London where he met with great success. West never returned to the colonies, but he welcomed young American artists to his studio. Among his many students were John Singleton Copley, Charles Willson Peale, Gilbert Stuart, John Trumbull, Thomas Sully, Samuel F. B. Morse, and Charles Bird King.

The Artist's Family, 1772, by Benjamin West. In this painting, West (far right) contrasted the fashionable London clothes worn by himself, his wife, and his son with the plain Quaker-style clothes of his father and brother

The first professional woman artist in America was Henrietta Johnston. She and her husband arrived in Charleston, South Carolina, about 1707. Though untrained as an artist, Johnston earned extra money by making portraits of the well-to-do. She worked in pastels, and her portraits, like the one she painted in 1711 of Henriette Charlotte Chastaigner, were simple and direct.

AN AMERICAN
Original

Henry Pelham (Boy with a Squirrel),
1765, by John Singleton Copley.
In this painting, Copley shows his 16-year-old
stepbrother holding a leash attached to a flying squirrel.

John Singleton Copley is considered the greatest artist of colonial America. He was born in Boston in 1738, the same year as Benjamin West. After Copley's father died, his mother married the engraver Peter Pelham. Copley had his first contact with the arts in Pelham's shop. He probably also saw the work of Pelham's partner, John Smibert.

At age 15, Copley began his career. He was skilled in capturing a good likeness, and before long he was able to support himself by painting portraits. Still, Copley wasn't happy. He knew he was good but wondered how his own work compared with the works of great European artists. In 1765, he painted *Henry Pelham (Boy with a Squirrel)* and sent it to be exhibited at the Society of Artists in London. Benjamin West saw the painting and wrote to Copley, suggesting he come and study in England. West thought Copley needed to become more skillful with light and shade so his work would not appear to be "liny."

Watson and the Shark, 1778, by John Singleton Copley. Among the rescuers in Copley's painting is an African-American man. It was one of the first times in American art that a black person was shown in a flattering manner.

Tensions were growing between the colonies and England. With the threat of war hanging over their heads, fewer people were ordering portraits. In 1774, Copley finally left the colonies. He settled in London and took up history painting. The most famous of these paintings was *Watson and the Shark*.

In 1749, Brooke Watson, a young sailor, lost his leg to a shark in the waters off Havana, Cuba. He recovered and by 1778, was a successful merchant in London. That year, probably at Watson's request, Copley painted him being attacked by the shark. It was one of the first history paintings that featured ordinary people.

CHAPTER 2

ON THE ROAD TO REVOLUTION

From early on, England had passed laws to control trade. The laws said what goods could be shipped to or from the colonies. This was to protect English industries, such as wool and molasses. The laws also said that goods had to be shipped in English or English-built ships. The colonists had to pay many taxes, and as early as 1687, settlers in Massachusetts protested taxation without representation.

Benjamin Franklin owned a print shop in Philadelphia. He wrote and published *Poor Richard's Almanack*, a kind of calendar with all sorts of useful information. In 1729, Franklin took over an ailing newspaper called the *Pennsylvania Gazette* and made it successful. In it, he published news as well as articles and cartoons about politics.

Portrait of Benjamin Franklin, 1789, by Charles Willson Peale. When Peale was hired to paint this portrait, Franklin was so sick he could only pose for a few minutes at a time. Peale's solution was to copy another portrait he'd painted in 1785 and simply update it.

After Franklin retired from printing, he went on to become an inventor, a scientist, a musician, and a statesman. Franklin invented bifocals, a freestanding cast-iron stove he called the Pennsylvania Fire Place (now known as the Franklin stove), and the lightning rod. He was the first to propose daylight saving time and map the Gulf Stream. Franklin founded Philadelphia's first public library, its first city hospital, and the University of Pennsylvania.

Franklin thought up the unusual name of *Poor Richard's Almanack*. He pretended someone named Richard Saunders wrote it. Saunders was said to be poor because his nagging wife spent all his money.

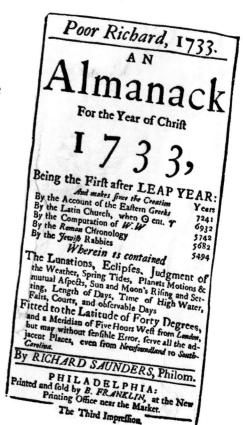

Benjamin Franklin drew the first political cartoon, "Join, or Die," which appeared in the *Pennsylvania Gazette* on May 9, 1754. It pictured a snake, and each section stood for a colony. Franklin's message was clear: In order to survive, the colonies had to unite with England against the French, who were claiming land in the Ohio River Valley. That same year, the colonists fought with England in the French and Indian War. At the end of it, the English owned all the land east of the Mississippi River except for New Orleans.

Paul Revere was a silversmith and printer in Boston. One night in 1770, a fight broke out between English soldiers and a crowd of troublemakers. In the confusion, the soldiers panicked and fired on the crowd. Five colonists died. Revere made a color engraving of the shootings that showed the British cold-bloodedly firing on the crowd.

It was not accurate, but it served to stir up anti-British feelings among the colonists.

Tea was one of the many items taxed by England. In 1773, some colonists dressed up as Native Americans and tossed chests of tea into Boston Harbor. King George ordered the harbor closed, and many colonists began to think of breaking away from England. Loyalists, or Tories, wanted to remain part of England. Patriots wanted to revolt and break free.

Paul Revere, 1768, by John Singleton Copley.
In this painting, Paul Revere is shown holding one of his silver teapots. Three of his engraving tools lie on the table.

In March 1775, Patrick Henry gave his famous speech in Virginia, which ended with the words,

"I know not what course others may take; but as for me, give me liberty or give me death!"

On April 19, 1775, the first shots of the American Revolution were fired at Lexington, Massachusetts.

Paul Revere based his engraving, called *The Bloody Massacre*, on a drawing by Henry Pelham. Though Pelham's print was a little more true to life, it came out almost two weeks after Revere's and did not sell as well.

Yankee Doodle went to town,
A-riding on a pony.
Stuck a feather in his cap
And called it Macaroni.

The British used the words *Yankee Doodle* for an American hick who couldn't fight. As the British army marched on Concord and Lexington, Massachusetts, "Yankee Doodle" was the song played by the drummers and pipers. After winning the two battles, the Americans claimed the song as their own. Both armies gave commands through music. This method let officers communicate quickly to whole armies.

CHAPTER 3

A new NATION

> *We hold these truths to be self-evident, that all men are created equal.*
>
> —Declaration of Independence, 1776

Created in 1819, this copy of the Declaration of Independence shows the state seals of the 13 original colonies as well as portraits of George Washington, John Hancock, and Thomas Jefferson.

Thomas Jefferson wrote the words at left as part of the Declaration of Independence. At the time, the word *men* stood for only white men. It would be many years after the Revolution before other Americans would have a say in their government. The Declaration was adopted by the Continental Congress on July 4, 1776, and by July 9, all 13 colonies had declared their independence from England.

John Trumbull had declared his own independence when he went against his father's wishes to become an artist. Early in the war, he served as an aide to General George Washington but left to continue his studies. In 1780, Trumbull went to London to study under Benjamin

West. There, Trumbull was arrested as a spy. West used his friendship with King George to help free Trumbull, who then returned to America. Trumbull supported himself by painting portraits, but he thought history painting was a higher calling. He spent many years painting the important people and events of the Revolution.

Declaration of Independence, 4 July 1776, by John Trumbull. The Declaration of Independence was actually signed on August 2, 1776. John Trumbull took the trouble to find 36 of the original 47 signers so he could paint them from life. This version is one of four murals Trumbull later painted for the Rotunda of the Capitol.

Mercy Otis Warren was a Patriot. Before the Revolution, she wrote unsigned plays mocking British policies and officials. As a woman, Warren could not take part in the new government, but she wrote hundreds of letters to Thomas Jefferson, Benjamin Franklin, and other officials. She also wrote poetry, and in 1805, when she was 77 years old, her three-volume *History of the Rise, Progress, and Termination of the American Revolution* was published.

Mrs. James Warren (Mercy Otis), 1763, by John Singleton Copley.

George Washington, 1796, by Gilbert Stuart. Washington posed for Stuart three times. Like many of Stuart's paintings, this well-known portrait of Washington was left unfinished.

In 1783, the American Revolution ended. The Constitution was adopted by the states and became law in 1788. In 1789, George Washington became the first president of the United States elected under the Constitution.

The nation's first capital was New York City and the second, Philadelphia. However, there were plans for a new capital. It would not be in any state, but on the Potomac River in the District of Columbia. Benjamin Banneker, a mathematician, astronomer, and a free African American, was appointed by President Washington to survey the land. Pierre Charles L'Enfant, a French architect who arrived in 1777 and fought in the war, was chosen to lay out the new capital.

Gilbert Stuart's family were loyalists who fled to Canada in 1775. Stuart went to London to study art under Benjamin West. There he became a successful portrait painter. In fact, he took on so much work, he couldn't finish it all and had to leave town. After a stay in Ireland, he returned to the United States. Portraits of George Washington were in great demand, and Stuart took advantage of this. He painted only three portraits of Washington from life, but used them as the basis for another 111 paintings.

Pierre Charles L'Enfant based his plans for the capital on the gardens of Versailles in France, where his father had worked as an artist for the king. First called Federal City, the capital was renamed Washington in 1791.

AMERICAN COOKERY:

OR, THE ART OF DRESSING

VIANDS, FISH, POULTRY, AND VEGETABLES.

AND THE BEST MODE OF MAKING

PUFF PASTES, PIES, TARTS, PUDDINGS, CUSTARDS AND PRESERVES.

AND ALL KINDS OF

CAKES,

FROM THE IMPERIAL PLUMB TO PLAIN CAKE.

Adapted to this country and all grades of life.

BY AN AMERICAN ORPHAN.

WALPOLE, N. H.
PRINTED FOR ELIJAH BROOKS.
1812.

The Power of Sympathy, the first American novel, appeared in 1789. It was written by William Hill Brown. Within the next 11 years, about 350 novels were published. The first best-seller was *Coquette*, by Hannah Webster Foster. *American Cookery*, by Amelia Simmons, was published in 1796. It was the first cookbook by an American author printed in the United States. Simmons included recipes using Native American ingredients, such as cornmeal and squash.

Thomas Jefferson, 1805, by Rembrandt Peale. Jefferson was 62 years old when Peale painted this portrait.

With the founding of the new country, the federal style of architecture became popular. It was adapted from the European **neoclassical** style, which was based on the architecture of Greece and Rome. It seemed fitting that architecture in the new democratic republic should look back to the democracies of ancient times.

Thomas Jefferson, the author of the Declaration of Independence and the third president of the United States, was also a farmer, a scientist, and an architect. In 1785, Jefferson was made minister to France. While living in Paris, he fell in love with the neoclassical style. After he returned home, he designed the state capitol of Virginia with the help of French architect Charles-Louis Clérisseau. The plans were based on an ancient Roman temple Jefferson had seen in Nîmes, France. Jefferson also redesigned Monticello, his own house in Virginia, modeled on the neoclassical homes he'd seen in Paris. Inside, he designed doors that seemed to swing open by themselves, **dumbwaiters**, and hidden staircases.

West Front of the United States Capitol, by John Rubens Smith, ca. 1830. In Smith's watercolor, cows graze near the almost completed Capitol building.

Benjamin Henry Latrobe and Charles Bulfinch were two of the architects who worked on the new Capitol building in Washington. Both Latrobe and Bulfinch designed in the federal style, but were inspired by neoclassical buildings in England rather than France. Latrobe adapted details to fit the new country. For example, he topped some of the columns of the Senate with tobacco flowers and leaves instead of the usual Greek acanthus leaves. Bulfinch designed the high dome of the Capitol rotunda.

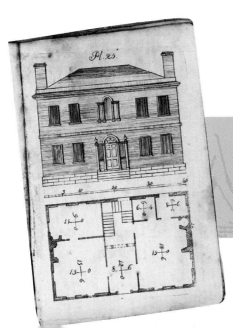

In 1797, Asher Benjamin published *The Country Builder's Assistant,* the first American pattern book. It was followed by several other books, including *The American Builder's Companion*. Benjamin's books included many of the American federal-style versions of English neoclassical designs.

CHAPTER 4

A NEW CENTURY

Exhumation of the Mastodon, 1860, by Charles Willson Peale. The man next to the pole in the center of the watery pit is showing a mastodon bone to Peale, who stands with his children on the right.

The early years of the new century saw many scientific discoveries and new inventions. Handmade goods began to be made by machine, and work was split up into separate tasks done by different workers. The nation grew in population and territory. Philadelphia and New York were busy cities where the arts thrived. In Washington, the Library of Congress was established in 1800. In 1805, Charles Willson Peale founded Philadelphia's Pennsylvania Academy of Fine Arts, where artists study to this day.

In 1801, Peale, who was a scientist as well as an artist, traveled to Newburgh, New York. He wanted to see the fossils of an unknown animal that had been found nearby. Excited by what he saw, he looked for enough bones to make a complete skeleton. In 1806, the skeleton was identified as belonging to a mastodon, an extinct ancestor of the elephant.

Sofa, ca. 1810–1820, attributed to Duncan Phyfe.

In 1803, President Jefferson doubled the nation's size by buying a giant piece of real estate—the Louisiana Territory—from the French. It cost 15 million dollars for almost 525 million acres, which comes out to about three cents per acre. Meriwether Lewis and William Clark were hired to lead an **expedition** to explore the new Northwest.

Born in Scotland, Duncan Phyfe came to America at age 15. He settled in New York, where he opened a furniture shop. Phyfe adapted his designs from English pattern books. As his business grew, Phyfe hired other people to build the furniture and later installed machines to help with the work. Instead of waiting for orders, Phyfe began to build ready-made furniture.

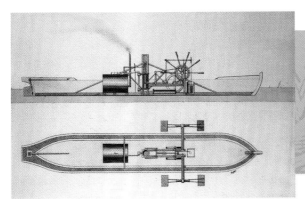

Robert Fulton was both an artist and an inventor. His paintings might not be remembered today, but his most famous invention—the steamboat—is. In 1807, the *Clermont*, the first of 16 steamboats he designed, sailed up the Hudson River. It took 32 hours for the ship to get from New York to Albany, a trip of 150 miles (241 km).

THE PAINTING Peales

The Artist in His Museum, 1822, by Charles Willson Peale.
To get many of the birds and animals for his museum, Peale did his own trapping and learned taxidermy. Part of the mastodon skeleton can be seen behind the curtain at the right.

Charles Willson Peale learned saddlery, sign painting, and several other trades before he decided to become a painter. He figured painting was a trade one could learn, just like any other. Though he took some lessons in Annapolis, Maryland, and later studied with Benjamin West in London, Peale was mostly self-taught.

In 1775, he settled in Philadelphia. After serving in the Revolutionary War, he painted portraits of its heroes, including many of his friend George Washington. In the mid-1780s, Peale opened the first public museum in the United States, where he displayed his portraits. His interest in natural history and science led Peale to exhibit "curiosities" as well. Among them were the mastodon skeleton he found in New York, stuffed animals and birds, and

Rubens Peale with a Geranium, 1801, by Rembrandt Peale. Rubens Peale, who was interested in botany, had poor vision and needed two pairs of glasses, one for seeing close up and one for distance.

artifacts from Lewis and Clark's exploration of the Louisiana Territory. By 1820, the museum contained more than 100,000 objects.

Peale also headed the first family of American painters. He had 17 children, 11 of whom lived to adulthood. Several were named after famous European artists and eight, including Raphaelle and Rembrandt, became professional artists.

After his study with West, Peale had taught what he learned to his younger brother James. James became a painter of still lifes and portraits, especially **miniatures**. Two of his daughters, Anna Claypoole and Sarah Miriam, also became professional artists. Anna painted miniatures while Sarah painted large-scale portraits of some of the most important people of the day, including the Marquis de Lafayette and Henry Wise, the governor of Virginia.

Elizabeth Bordley Polk Bend (Mrs. Joseph Grove Bend), ca. 1820–1830, by Anna Claypoole Peale. Miniature portraits were popular because their small size allowed them to be easily carried, almost like snapshots are today.

> *"O! Say, can you see, by the dawn's early light, What so proudly we hail'd at the twilight's last gleaming?*
>
> —From "The Star Spangled Banner," by Francis Scott Key

By 1812, America was back at war with England. In 1815, Americans fought a battle defending Fort McHenry in Baltimore, Maryland. Francis Scott Key, a lawyer, had gone aboard a British ship to discuss the release of an American prisoner. He watched the battle, and as dawn came, he saw the American flag waving over the fort. The British had lost the battle. Inspired, Key wrote a poem called "The Defense of Fort McHenry." Today, most Americans know it as "The Star Spangled Banner," our national anthem.

Washington Irving lived just north of New York City and wrote books under different pen

The words to "The Star Spangled Banner" are sung to the tune of an old English drinking song.

names. Under Diedrich Knickerbocker, he wrote funny stories about the Dutch of New York. In 1820, he published *The Sketch Book of Geoffrey Crayon*, a collection of sketches, or stories. Many of the stories, including "The Legend of Sleepy Hollow" and "Rip Van Winkle," are still well known today.

Washington Irving was named after his parents' hero, George Washington.

Whaling had been a part of New England life since the days of the early colonists. Between whale sightings, sailors were often left with a lot of free time on their hands. To keep busy, they carved whale jawbones and teeth. They made practical things, such as handles and boxes, but they also carved pictures, which were called scrimshaw.

Pat Lyon at the Forge, 1826–27, by John Neagle.
When Lyon was young, he was falsely accused of bank robbery and thrown in Philadelphia's Walnut Street Jail. In the painting, the cupola of the jail is visible through the window.

In the early 1800s, English-born Thomas Sully became the most popular portrait artist in Philadelphia. He worked in the romantic style, painting men as handsome and carefree, and women as sweet and pretty. Sully's son-in-law, John Neagle, was also a painter. His most famous painting is of Pat Lyon, a wealthy Irishman. Lyon posed as a blacksmith, the trade he practiced when young. This was to show that in America it was possible for someone who started out poor to become rich.

Today, Samuel F. B. Morse is known as the inventor of the telegraph and Morse Code, but he was also an artist. Like others before him, Morse thought young artists suffered because there were so few good teachers and works of art to see in America. Along with artist Thomas Cole and architect Ithiel Town, Morse organized the National Academy of Design in New York City in 1826 and was its first president. After getting the idea for the telegraph, Morse gave up painting and devoted the rest of his life to science.

Folk artists were untrained and did not concern themselves with the styles of the day. Many painted for pleasure. Some, like Ammi Phillips, traveled from town to town painting portraits to earn a living. Phillips traveled throughout New York, Connecticut, and Massachusetts. Sometimes he painted the portraits of every member in a household.

Portrait of a Girl in a Red Dress, 1834–36, by Ammi Phillips

By 1830, New York City was America's financial center as well as its biggest city and major port. This was partly due to its great harbor and the opening of the Erie Canal in 1825. The canal linked the Hudson River to Lake Erie, making it easier to reach the Midwest. Boats carrying up to 30 tons of freight were pulled upriver by oxen on towpaths along the canal's banks. Passenger boats were pulled by horses or mules.

View on the Erie Canal, 1830–32, by John William Hill

"'Twas the night before Christmas," begins "A Visit from St. Nicholas." Clement Clarke Moore, a teacher and scholar in New York City, wrote this fanciful poem as a gift for his children. Although he didn't mean for it to be published, it somehow found its way into print. *The Troy Sentinel* published the poem on December 23, 1823, without Moore's name.

A Visit from St. Nicholas. 125

Clement Clarke Moore's poem, "A Visit from St. Nicholas," helped give Saint Nicholas a new image as a jolly elf, as later drawn by Thomas Nast.

Moore did not admit to writing the poem until 1844.

"We wish to plead our own cause. Too long have others spoken for us." These words were printed on the front page of *Freedom's Journal*, the first African-American newspaper. The four-page weekly was started in 1827 by a group of free black men in New York City. It ran in 11 states, as well as Europe, Canada, and Haiti.

In the early 1800s, there weren't many public schools. Those that did exist were usually crowded one-room schoolhouses with poorly trained teachers and few textbooks. After attending Yale University, Noah Webster became a schoolteacher. In 1783, unhappy with the textbooks he had to use, Webster wrote *A Grammatical Institute of the English Language*. Because of its blue cover, it was also called the "Blue-backed Speller."

At that time, not all Americans used, spelled, or pronounced words the same way. Webster wanted that to change. In 1828, he published *An American Dictionary of the English Language*. Webster used American spellings and added American words, such as *applesauce* and *squash*.

Noah Webster, the Schoolmaster of the Republic, ca. 1891.
It took Noah Webster more than 20 years to research and write the first American dictionary, which defined about 70,000 words.

On February 7, 1827, Francisque Hutin, a French dancer, **pirouetted** before a crowded audience in New York City. It was the first time ballet was performed in the United States. Hutin's short costume shocked many members of the audience because women of that time wore long skirts and petticoats. In 1838, Augusta Maywood (left), the first American ballerina, danced in *La Bayadére* when she was just 12 years old.

RED JACKET.
SENECA WAR CHIEF.

Published by Campbell and Burns

Red Jacket, Seneca War Chief, ca. 1835, from a painting by Charles Bird King.

Early American whites had mixed views of Native Americans. Some thought of them as "noble savages." Others saw them as simply savages. In fact, white settlers moved in on Native American land, changed or destroyed their way of life, and brought diseases that killed millions.

Superintendent of Indian Trade Thomas McKenney was supportive of Native Americans. In 1821, he hired Charles Bird King to paint portraits for an "Indian Gallery." Most were chiefs who had traveled to Washington, D.C., on tribal business. Between 1821 and 1842, King painted 143 of their portraits. In 1830, President Andrew Jackson fired McKenney. After that, he worked on publishing a collection of hand-colored lithographs (prints), mostly of King's paintings. The three-volume set of *The Indian Tribes of North America with Biographical Sketches and Anecdotes of the Principal Chiefs* appeared in 1837. Without these lithographs, most of King's work would have been lost. All but three of his original paintings burned in a fire in 1865.

The Bear Dance, 1844, by George Catlin. Catlin not only painted portraits but also recorded a disappearing way of life.

A self-taught artist, George Catlin saw and painted Native Americans passing through Philadelphia on their way to Washington, D.C. Not content with only studio portraits, Catlin wanted to visit "every nation of Indians on the Continent of North America." He set off in 1830 and, with the help of William Clark, visited 50 tribes by 1836.

Unlike earlier presidents who were from well-to-do families, Andrew Jackson was a self-made man. During his inauguration, well-wishers streamed into the White House to get a better look at their new president. Jackson was a great believer in democracy but not for Native Americans, whom he once called "savage bloodhounds." Under his presidency, the Indian Removal Act forced thousands of eastern Native Americans to move west of the Mississippi River.

President's Levee, or All Creation Going to the White House, 1841, by Robert Cruikshank.

CHAPTER 5

WILDERNESS AND THE ARTS

Carolina Parakeet, ca. 1825, by John James Audubon. The Carolina parakeet was the only parakeet native to the United States. This once common bird became extinct in the early 1900s, due to overhunting.

At age 18, John James Audubon arrived in America from France. Even as a child, Audubon had enjoyed drawing birds. Audubon married and started several businesses, but when they all failed, he decided to become a full-time artist. He planned to paint a series of life-size birds in their natural setting and publish it with descriptions. A natural outdoorsman, Audubon took off for the woods for months at a time. He didn't have good telescopes or cameras with zoom lenses. To see the birds close up, he had to shoot them. Then he wired the bodies in the poses he wanted to paint.

In 1824, Audubon began to look for a publisher for *The Birds of America* in Philadelphia but no one was interested. In 1826, he went to England. There he worked with engravers Robert J. Havell, his son, and as many as 50 watercolorists to create 40- by 20-inch (102 by 66 cm) hand-colored prints of his paintings. It took ten years to create 435 prints, which were published in 87 parts of five prints each.

Considered the father of American **entomology**, Thomas Say published his three-volume *American Entomology: or Descriptions of the Insects of North America* beginning in 1824. The books were illustrated by Say and Titian Ramsey Peale, the youngest son of Charles Willson Peale.

Saturnia promethea,1833, by Titian Ramsey Peale. This color plate appeared in a pamphlet advertising *The Butterflies of North America*. Unfortunately, the book was never completed.

James Fenimore Cooper wrote adventure stories about the frontier. *The Last of the Mohicans*, published in 1826, was his most popular work. The novel is set during the War of 1812, and its hero is Natty Bumppo, a wilderness scout and frontiersman. Cooper wrote five books about Bumppo, which are known as the Leatherstocking tales.

The Last of the Mohicans, 1826, by Thomas Cole.

Go forth under the open sky, and list to Nature's teachings,
while from all around—Earth and her waters, and the
depths of air—Comes a still voice—
—From "Thanatopsis," by William Cullen Bryant

Most Americans in the early 1800s looked at the wilderness as territory to be tamed. Rivers, forests, and other natural resources were there for people to use as needed. Some Americans, however, saw untamed nature as a source of spiritual renewal. The timeless natural wonders of the wilderness took the place of Europe's ancient castles and ruins. America's wilderness was part of its identity, and many artists began to paint landscapes.

One of these artists was Thomas Cole, who came to Philadelphia from England in 1818. After seeing the work of Gilbert Stuart and Thomas Sully, Cole decided to become a painter. Though he had no formal training, he became America's first major landscape artist. Most of Cole's landscape paintings were scenes of New York's Catskill Mountains and Hudson River Valley, and of New England.

The Falls of Kaaterskill, 1826, by Thomas Cole.
When Cole painted Kaaterskill Falls, he chose to include a Native American, though there were few left in the area, and to leave out the stairs and viewing tower that had been built for visitors.

Today, Cole is known as the leader of the Hudson River School, a group of artists whose work celebrated the American landscape. These artists often used special lighting effects to add drama to their landscapes, a technique called luminism. Over the next 50 years, they painted landscapes of the wilderness from upstate New York west to California. Among them were Asher B. Durand, Frederic Edwin Church, and Albert Bierstadt.

During the 1800s, literature, too, celebrated nature. In 1836, Ralph Waldo Emerson published *Nature*, a collection of essays that championed living simply and in harmony with nature. Later, Henry David Thoreau would take this idea even further in his famous book, *Walden*.

William Cullen Bryant's poem "Thanatopsis" was published in 1817.

In just over 200 years, the new country had gone from a few tiny colonies along the Atlantic coast to a republic whose borders stretched all the way to the Pacific. Its thriving Eastern cities were centers of art and culture, with museums, libraries, theaters, and colleges. From only a few artists and architects imitating the styles of Europe, there were now many professionals, who were forging their own distinctive styles. The United States had become a force to be reckoned with, in both the art world and the wider world.

1565   Spanish settlers found St. Augustine, Florida

1585   First British colonists settle Roanoke Island, Virginia

1607   British colonists settle Jamestown, Virginia

1609   Henry Hudson claims the Hudson River area for the Dutch

ca. 1612   Anne Bradstreet born (d. 1672)

1619   First Africans brought to Virginia by force and enslaved

1620   Plymouth Colony founded in Massachusetts

1630   Massachusetts Bay Colony founded

1674   New Netherland falls to the British and becomes New York

1635   First public school founded in Boston

1636   Harvard College founded in Boston

1640   First book printed and published in the colonies

1674   Henrietta Johnston born (d. 1729)

1688   John Smibert born (d. 1751)

ca. 1695   Peter Pelham born (d. 1751)

1706   Benjamin Franklin born (d. 1790)

1720   Charles-Louis Clérisseau born (d. 1820)

1728   Mercy Otis Warren born (d. 1814)

1731   Benjamin Banneker born (d. 1806)

1732   George Washington born (d. 1799)

1735   Paul Revere born (d. 1818)

1736   Patrick Henry born (d. 1799)

1738   Benjamin West born (d. 1820); John S. Copley born (d. 1815)

1741   Charles Willson Peale born (d. 1827)

1743   Thomas Jefferson born (d. 1826)

1749   James Peale born (d. 1831)

1754   French and Indian War begins (ends 1763); Pierre Charles L'Enfant born (d. 1852)

1755   Gilbert Stuart born (d. 1828)

1756   John Trumbull born (d. 1843)

1758   Noah Webster born (d. 1843); Hannah Webster Foster born (d.1840)

1763   Charles Bulfinch born (d. 1844)

1764   Benjamin Henry Latrobe born (d. 1820)

1765   William Hill Brown born (d. 1793); Robert Fulton born (d. 1815)

1767   Andrew Jackson born (d. 1845)

1768   Duncan Phyfe born (d. 1854)

1770   The Boston Massacre takes place; William Clark born (d. 1838)

1773   The Boston Tea Party takes place; Asher Benjamin born (d. 1845)

1774   Meriwether Lewis born (d. 1809); Raphaelle Peale born (d. 1825)

1775   American Revolution begins (ends 1783)

1776   Declaration of Independence adopted by Continental Congress

1778   Rembrandt Peale born (d. 1860)

1779   Clement Clarke Moore born (d. 1863); Francis Scott Key born (d. 1843)

1783   Thomas Sully born (d. 1872); Washington Irving born (d. 1859)

1785   Charles Bird King born (d. 1862); Thomas McKenney born (d. 1859); John James Audubon born (d. 1851)

1787   Thomas Say born (d. 1834)

1788   Ammi Phillips born (d. 1865)

1789   The Constitution becomes law; George Washington elected president; James Fenimore Cooper born (d. 1851)

1791   Samuel F. B. Morse born (d. 1872); Anna C. Peale born (d. 1878)

1794   William Cullen Bryant born (d. 1878)

1796   John Neagle born (d. 1865); George Catlin born (d. 1872); Asher B. Durand born (d. 1886)

1799   Titian Ramsey Peale born (d. 1885)

1800   Library of Congress established in Washington, D.C.; Sarah Miriam Peale born (d. 1885)

1801   Thomas Jefferson elected president; Thomas Cole born (d. 1848)

1803   Ralph Waldo Emerson born (d. 1882)

1803   Louisiana Territory becomes part of the United States

1807   First steamboat sails from New York City to Albany

1812   The War of 1812 begins (ends 1815)

1817   Henry David Thoreau born (d. 1862)

1825   Erie Canal opens; Augusta Maywood born (d. 1876)

1828   Andrew Jackson elected president

1830   Indian Removal Act passed; Albert Bierstadt born (d. 1902

artifact an object remaining from an earlier time period

distinct different from other styles or things

dumbwaiter a type of mini elevator used to move food from one floor to another

engraving a print made by cutting letters, designs, or pictures into blocks or plates; a person who makes such a print is an engraver

entomology the study of insects

exception someone or something to which a rule does not apply

expedition a group of people who make a journey for a special reason; also the journey

history painting a painting that captures an important or dramatic event from history or literature; also the act of creating such a painting

indentured servant a person who signs a contract agreeing to work for someone for a certain number of years in return for travel expenses as well as room and board

limner an old word for a painter, especially a portrait painter

miniature a very small painting, usually a portrait

neoclassical an architectural, artistic, musical, or literary style that refers back to ancient Greece and Rome

notable worthy of note, often well-known

Old Master an artwork by a masterful painter, usually from the 1500s to the early 1700s; also the artist who created such a work

partnership two or more people who contract to work together

pastel a chalklike drawing stick; also the picture made with such drawing sticks

pirouette to spin in a circle while balancing on the toe or ball of one foot; also, the spin itself

prosper thrive

status someone's position in relation to others

upholster the materials used to make a soft back or seat for a piece of furniture; also the act of making such a back or seat

worldly something unrelated to religious or spiritual matters

Joan Blos, *A Gathering of Days: A New England Girl's Journal*, 1830–32, Simon & Schuster, 1990

Robert Burleigh, *Into the Woods: John James Audubon Lives His Dream*, Simon & Schuster, 2003

Leonard Everett Fisher, *The Limners: America's Earliest Portrait Painters* (Colonial Craftsmen), Benchmark Books, 2000

Candace Fleming, *Ben Franklin's Almanac: Being a True Account of the Good Gentleman's Life*, Atheneum/Anne Schwartz Books, 2003

Mary Rodd Furbee, *Outrageous Women of Colonial America* (Outrageous Women), Wiley, 2001

Ann McGovern and Brinton Turkle, *If You Lived in Colonial Times*, Scholastic, 1992

Richard Panchyk, *American Folk Art for Kids: With 21 Activities*, Chicago Review Press, 2004

Janet Wilson, *The Ingenious Mr. Peale: Painter, Patriot, and Man of Science*, Atheneum, 1996

Web Sites
Early American Paintings in the
Worcester Art Museum, Worcester, Massachusetts
http://www.worcesterart.org/Collection/Early_American

PBS: Colonial House
http://www.pbs.org/wnet/colonialhouse

The Star-Spangled Banner:
The Flag That Inspired the National Anthem
Smithsonian, National Museum of American History
http://web8.si.edu/nmah/htdocs/ssb-old/6_thestory/6b_osay/main6b.html

The editors wish to thank the following organizations and individuals for permission to reprint the literary quotes and to reproduce the images in this book. Every effort has been made to obtain permission from the owners of all materials. Any errors that may have been made are unintentional and will be corrected in future printings if notice is given to the publisher.

Cover: *The Peaceable Kingdom,* c. 1833 (oil on canvas), Edward Hicks (1780–1849)/© Worcester Art Museum, Massachusetts/Bridgeman Art Library
Title page: William Russell Birch/*A View of the Capitol,* ca. 1800/Library of Congress
p. 4: Powder horn inscribed with map, ca. 1757/Library of Congress/Geography & Map Division
p. 5: Edward Savage/*Liberty in the Form of the Goddess of Youth: Giving Support to the Bald Eagle*/Stipple engraving on cream laid paper/1925.1045/Worcester Art Museum, Worcester, Massachusetts, gift of Mrs. Kingsmill Mars
p. 6: p. 6: John White/*Village of Secoton,* 1585/Watercolor/The Art Archive/British Museum/Eileen Tweedy
p. 7: *The Arrival of the Englishmen in Virginia,* 1590, engraving by Theodor de Bry/The Art Archive/Musée de la Marine, Paris/Dagli Orti
p. 8: American/*Elizabeth Clarke Freake (Mrs. John Freake) and Baby Mary*/Oil on canvas/1963.134/Worcester Art Museum, Worcester, Massachusetts, Gift of Mr. and Mrs. Albert W. Rice
p. 9 (top): Press Cupboard, 1710–1720, oak and pine, painted/Used by Hannah Barnard of Hadley, Massachusetts/From the Collections of The Henry Ford (36.178.1/G3369); **(bottom):** Photograph of Elizabeth Raynsford tombstone © Emily Sper/www.emilysper.com
p. 10: Harvard campus, 1726, engraving by Burgis/Library of Congress
p. 11: Facsimile title page for *The Whole Booke of Psalmes Faithfully Translated into English Metre,* 1640/Woodcut with watercolor wash/© North Wind/North Wind Picture Archives/All rights reserved;
p. 12: John Ward House/Photo by Louis Procopio/Courtesy of www.hawthorneinsalem.org
p. 13 (top): Justus Engelhardt Kühn/*Henry Darnall III (as a child)*/Oil on Canvas/1912.1.3/The Maryland Historical Society, Baltimore, Maryland; **(bottom):** The Wren Chapel/Photograph © 2005 Dr. Ellen K. Rudolph/www.drellenrudolph.com
p. 14: John Smibert/*George Berkeley* (1685–1753), 1727?/Oil on canvas, 192.9 x 75.6 cm (40 1/2 x 29 3/4 in.)/Gift of the Morris and Gwendolyn Cafritz Foundation/National Portrait Gallery, Smithsonian Institution/Art Resource, NY
p. 15 (top): *The Artist's Family* (oil on canvas), Benjamin West (1738–1820)/© Yale Center for British Art, Paul Mellon Collection, USA/Bridgeman Art Library; **(bottom):** *Henriette Charlotte Chastaigner* (1700–1754), 1711, by Henrietta De Beaulieu Dering Johnston (ca. 1674–1729), pastel on paper, Gibbes Museum of Art/Carolina Art Association, 1938.20.04
p. 16: John Singleton Copley, American, 1738–1815/*Henry Pelham (Boy with a Squirrel),* 1765/Oil on canvas/77.15 x 63.82 cm (30 3/8 x 25 1/8 in.)/Museum of Fine Arts, Boston/Gift of the artist's great granddaughter, 1978.297
p. 17: John Singleton Copley/*Watson and the Shark,* 1778, oil on canvas/Ferdinand Lammot Belin Fund/1963.6.1.(1906)/Image © Board of Trustees, National Gallery of Art, Washington, DC

p. 18: *Portrait of Benjamin Franklin* (1706–90), 1789 (oil on canvas), Charles Willson Peale (1741–1827)/© Atwater Kent Museum, Philadelphia/Bridgeman Art Library
p. 19 (top): Facsimile title page of 1733 *Poor Richard's Almanack*/Woodcut with a watercolor wash/Copyright © North Wind/North Wind Picture Archives. All rights reserved; **(bottom):** "Join, or Die"/May 9, 1754/Library of Congress
p. 20: John Singleton Copley, American, 1738–1815/*Paul Revere,* 1768/Oil on canvas/89.22 x 72.39 cm (35 1/8 x 28 1/2 in.)/Museum of Fine Arts, Boston/Gift of Joseph W. Revere, William B. Revere and Edward H. R. Revere, 30.781
p. 21 (top): *The Bloody Massacre,* 1700, engraving by Paul Revere/The Library of Congress; **(bottom):** Yankee Doodle 1776, by Archibald M. Willard (1836–1918)/Published ca. 1876/Library of Congress
p. 22: Facsimile Declaration of Independence, 1819, designed by John Binns (1772–1860)/Library of Congress
p. 23 (top): Declaration of Independence, by John Trumbull/Architect of the Capitol/Negative #70222; **(bottom):** John Singleton Copley, American, 1738–1815/*Mrs. James Warren (Mercy Otis),* about 1763/Oil on canvas/126.05 x 100.33 cm (49 5/8 x 39 1/2 in.)/Museum of Fine Arts, Boston/Bequest of Winslow Warren, 31.212
p. 24: Gilbert Stuart, American 1755–1828/*George Washington,* 1796/Oil on canvas/121.28 x 93.98 cm (47 3/4 x 37 in.)/Museum of Fine Arts, Boston/William Francis Warden Fund, John H. and Ernestine A. Payne Fund, Commonwealth Cultural Preservation Trust. Jointly owned by the Museum of Fine Arts, Boston, and the National Portrait Gallery, Washington, D.C., 1980.1
p. 25 (top): First printed edition of Pierre Charles L'Enfant's plan of the city of Washington, D.C., 1792/Library of Congress; **(bottom):** *American Cookery,* 1796, Amelia Simmons/Courtesy of the Morse Department of Special Collections, Hale Library, Kansas State University
p. 26: Rembrandt Peale/*Thomas Jefferson,* 1805/The Art Archive/Laurie Platt Winfrey
p. 27 (top): John Rubens Smith (1775–1849)/*West Front of the United States Capitol,* ca. 1830/watercolor on paper/Library of Congress; **(bottom):** Page from *The Country Builder's Assistant,* by Asher Benjamin/University of Delaware Library, Newark, Delaware
p. 28: Charles Willson Peale (1741–1827)/*Exhumation of the Mastadon,* ca. 1806–1808/Oil on Canvas/BCLM MA5911/The Maryland Historical Society, Baltimore, Maryland
p. 29 (top): *Sofa,* American. Attributed to Duncan Phyfe (Scottish, 1768–1854), ca. 1810–20. Mahogany, tulip poplar, cane, gilded brass. H. 34 in. L. 84 3/4 in. D. 23 3/4 in. (86.4 x 215.3 x 60.3 cm)/The Metropolitan Museum of Art, Gift of C. Ruxton Love Jr., 1960. (60.41) Photograph © 1980 The Metropolitan Museum of Art; **(bottom):** *Robert Fulton Paddle Steamer,* 18th-century watercolor/The Art Archive/Musée de la Marine, Paris/Dagli Orti
p. 30: Charles Willson Peale/*The Artist in His Museum,* 1822/Oil on canvas/103 3/4 x 79 7/8 in. [263.5 x 202.9 cm]/1878.1.2/Courtesy of the Pennsylvania Academy of the Fine Arts, Philadelphia/Gift of Mrs. Sarah Harrison (The Joseph Harrison, Jr. Collection)

p. 31 (top): Rembrandt Peale/*Rubens Peale with a Geranium,* 1801, oil on canvas/Patrons' Permanent Fund/1985.59.1./PA/Image © Board of Trustees, National Gallery of Art, Washington, DC; **(bottom):** Anna Claypoole Peale (1797–1878)/*Elizabeth Bordley Polk Bend (Mrs. Joseph Grove Bend)* (1770–1831), ca. 1820–1830/Watercolor on Ivory/1933.2.2/The Maryland Historical Society, Baltimore, Maryland
p. 32: Cover of sheet music for "The Star-Spangled Banner," ca. 1861/The Library of Congress
p. 33 (top): *Washington Irving,* ca. 1873/Steel engraving after painting by Alonzo Chappel/Library of Congress; **(bottom):** "The Susan on the Coast of Japan" Scrimshaw (tooth), American School (19th century)/Private Collection, Boltin Picture Library/Bridgeman Art Library
p. 34: John Neagle, American, 1796–1865/*Pat Lyon at the Forge,* 1826–27/Oil on canvas/238.12 x 172.72 cm (93 3/4 x 68 in.)/Museum of Fine Arts, Boston/Henry H. and Zoe Oliver Sherman Fund, 975.806
p. 35 (top): *Portrait of a Girl in a Red Dress,* Ammi Phillips (1788–1865)/Christie's Images/Bridgeman Art Library; **(bottom):** J. W. Hill/*View on the Erie Canal,* 1829/Watercolor/54577/I. N. Phelps Stokes Collection, Miriam and Ira D. Wallach Division, Prints and Photographs, The New York Public Library, Astor, Lenox and Tilden Foundations
p. 36: Thomas Nast/*Santa Claus*/First published 1863–64/The Art Archive/Culver Pictures
p. 37 (top): *Noah Webster, The Schoolmaster of the Republic,* ca. 1891/The Library of Congress; **(bottom):** Augusta Maywood, *La Bayadere* (as Isolde)/Jerome Robbins Dance Division, The New York Public Library for the Performing Arts, Astor, Lenox and Tilden Foundations
p. 38: *Red Jacket, Seneca War Chief,* ca. 1835, from a painting by Charles Bird King/The Library of Congress
p. 39 (top): George Catlin/*The Bear Dance,* 1844/Hand-colored lithograph printed by Haghe and Day, London/The Art Archive/Gift of Mrs. Sidney T. Miller/Buffalo Bill Historical Center, Cody, Wyoming/21.74.18; **(bottom):** Robert Cruikshank/*President's Levee, or All Creation Going to the White House,* 1841/Library of Congress
p. 41 (top): Titian Ramsey Peale/*Lepidoptera Americana,* 1833, Plate 3 *(Saturnia promethea)*/The Academy of Natural Sciences of Philadelphia, Ewell Sale Stewart Library; **(bottom):** Thomas Cole (1801–48), scene from *The Last of the Mohicans* by James Fenimore Cooper (1789–1851), published 1826 (oil on canvas)/Fenimore Art Museum, Cooperstown, New York/Bridgeman Art Library
p. 42: Thomas Cole/*The Falls of Kaaterskill*/From the Warner Collection of Gulf States Paper Corporation, on view in The Westervelt-Warner Museum of art, Tuscaloosa, AL
p. 43: *William Cullen Bryant,* ca. 1876/The Library of Congress
Backgrounds, pp. 4, 10–11, 18–19, 21, 32, 34, 42–43: Ablestock
Backgrounds, pp. 6–7, 8–9, 22, 25, 38: Library of Congress